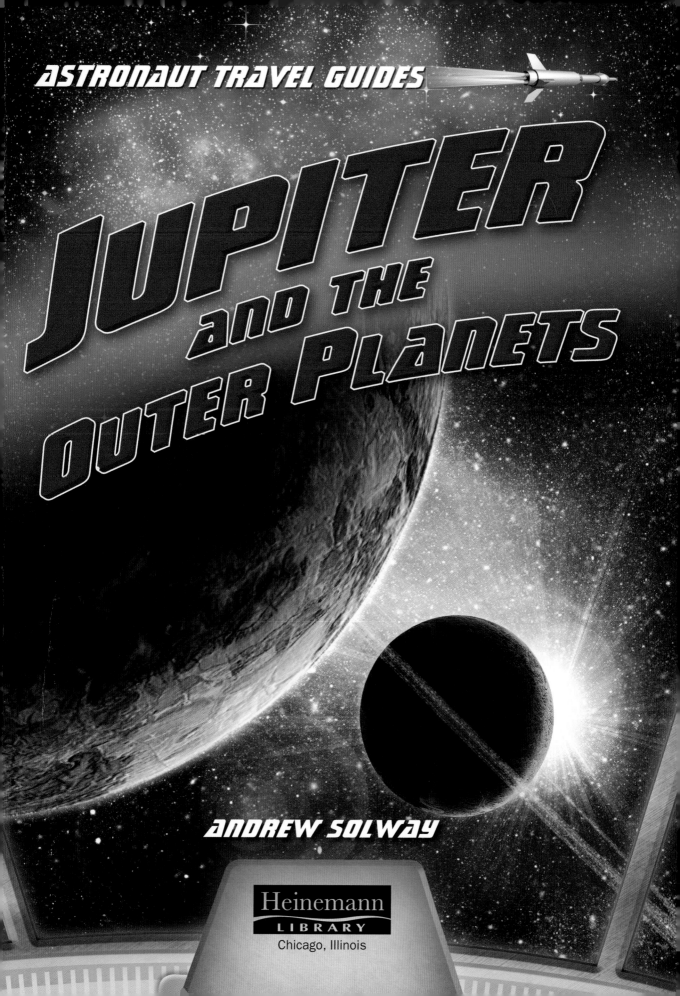

ASTRONAUT TRAVEL GUIDES

JUPITER
and the
OUTER PLANETS

ANDREW SOLWAY

Heinemann
LIBRARY
Chicago, Illinois

www.capstonepub.com
Visit our website to find out more information about Heinemann-Raintree books.

To order:
☎ Phone 800-747-4992
💻 Visit www.capstonepub.com
to browse our catalog and order online.

Edited by Nancy Dickmann and Laura Knowles
Designed by Steve Mead
Original illustrations © Capstone Global Library Ltd 2013
Picture research by Mica Brancic

Originated by Capstone Global Library Ltd
Printed and bound in the USA
in North Mankato, MN.
072013   007558RP

16 15 14 13
10 9 8 7 6 5 4

Library of Congress Cataloging-in-Publication Data
Solway, Andrew.
   Jupiter and the outer planets / Andrew Solway.—1st ed.
      p. cm.—(Astronaut travel guides)
   Includes bibliographical references and index.
   ISBN 978-1-4109-4569-3 (hb)—ISBN 978-1-4109-4578-5 (pb) 1. Jupiter (Planet)—Juvenile literature. 2. Planets—Juvenile literature. I. Title.
   QB661.S655 2013

   523.45—dc23   2011038992

Acknowledgements
We would like to thank the following for permission to reproduce photographs: Corbis p. 33; European Southern Observatory (ESO) p. 28 (L. Calçada); iStockphoto p. 6 (© Mikhail Khromov); John Spencer p. 20; NASA pp. 10 (JPL/University of Arizona), 11 (Goddard Space Flight Center Scientific Visualization Studio), 12 (Planetary Photojournal), 14 (JPL-Caltech/Space Science Institute), 15, 16 (Steven Hobbs (Brisbane, Queensland, Australia)), 17 (JPL/SSI), 18 (JPL/Space Science Institute), 19 (JPL/Space Science Institute), 24 (JPL/STScI), 25 (Ames Research Center), 26 (Jet Propulsion Laboratory), 36 (Johns Hopkins University Applied Physics Laboratory/Southwest Research Institute (JHUAPL/SwRI)), 37 (JPL), 39 (ESA - AOES Medialab), 5 bottom and 34, 5 middle and 31 (JPL/Caltech), 5 top and 27 (JPL/USGS); Science Photo Library pp. 4 (John Sanford), 8 (Friedrich Saurer), 22 (PAUL D STEWART); Shutterstock pp. 40-41 (© Martiin || Fluidworkshop).

Design image elements reproduced with permission of Shutterstock/© Andrea Danti/© Argus/© James Steidl/© Kyle Smith/© photobank.kiev.ua.

Cover photograph of a planet with rings at sunrise on the background of the cosmos reproduced with permission of Shutterstock/© Molodec.

We would like to thank John Spencer, Paolo Nespoli, and ESA for their invaluable help in the preparation of this book.

Every effort has been made to contact copyright holders of material reproduced in this book. Any omissions will be rectified in subsequent printings if notice is given to the publisher.

CONTENTS

Some words are shown in bold, **like this**. You can find out what they mean by looking in the glossary.

DON'T FORGET

These boxes will remind you what you need to take with you on your big adventure.

NUMBER CRUNCHING

Don't miss these little chunks of data as you speed through the travel guide!

AMAZING FACTS

You need to know these fascinating facts to get the most out of your space safari!

WHO'S WHO?

Find out about the space explorers who have studied the universe in the past and today.

WHERE ARE WE GOING?

In just two days, you are setting out on the trip of a lifetime. You will travel farther into space than anyone has been before. It's scary, isn't it? But it's exciting, too.

You are going on a trip to the outer planets. These are the **gas** giants of the **solar system**. The biggest, Jupiter, is absolutely huge. You could fit nearly 1,000 Earths inside it. Saturn, Uranus, and Neptune are also much bigger than Earth.

Jupiter

Mars

Saturn

Venus

Mercury

DON'T FORGET

Pack a spacesuit to protect you from the freezing temperatures. Most places you visit will be much colder than your freezer.

Sometimes five of the planets in the solar system can be seen in the night sky at the same time.

On your journey, you will get close to the gas giants, but you will not land. The main reason is that there isn't anything to land on! All the outer planets are made mostly of gas, although their cores are probably liquid. However, there are plenty of rocky moons where you might be able to land.

HOW FAR?

This trip is not short! Neptune is about 2.7 billion miles (4.4 billion kilometers) from Earth, and you will need to make detours to visit the other planets. The **space probe** *Voyager 2* took 12 years to make the trip. So pack some good books and games!

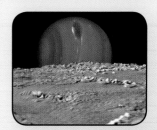

Discover which of Neptune's moons would be the best to visit on page 25.

Turn to page 31 to find out how to power your spaceship.

Meet astronaut Paolo Nespoli on page 34.

AMAZING FACTS

Your trip will take a route similar to the one taken by the *Voyager* space probes. *Voyager 1* flew to Jupiter and Saturn. *Voyager 2* visited Jupiter, Saturn, Uranus, and Neptune. They are still flying and sending signals back to Earth, even though they are billions of miles away.

THE OUTER PLANETS

All the outer planets are named after Roman and Greek gods. So are most of their moons. **Astronomers** have known about Jupiter and Saturn since ancient times, but Uranus and Neptune were discovered more recently.

JUPITER

Jupiter is a good name for the biggest planet, because Jupiter was the leader of the Roman gods. You cannot always see Jupiter in the night sky, but when you can, it is one of the brightest objects. The biggest feature on Jupiter is called the Great Red Spot. The spot may first have been seen in 1665. We now know that it is a giant storm.

Jupiter was believed to be a god of the sky and was often shown holding a thunderbolt.

SATURN

Saturn is named after the Roman god of farming, who was Jupiter's father. The two planets were named after father and son because they were seen as being closely related. Saturn is best known for its amazing rings. The first person to see them was Galileo Galilei in 1610. In 1655, Dutch scientist Christiaan Huygens became the first person to recognize that they were rings.

URANUS

Uranus was discovered by British astronomer William Herschel in 1781. Astronomers named Jupiter after the Greek god of the heavens. The planet is only just visible with the human eye, but it is very difficult to see from Earth without a **telescope**.

NEPTUNE

Neptune was the Roman god of the oceans. The planet was given this name because of its sea-blue color. Astronomers predicted that Neptune must exist before it was actually found. It was first seen in 1846. It is the only planet in the solar system that is invisible to the human eye.

DON'T FORGET

In space, your muscles do not need to work against **gravity**, so they quickly get weak. Don't forget to take along an exercise bike and some weights, so you can keep your muscles in shape.

THE BIGGEST GIANT

The first part of your trip will take you past Mars and through the **asteroid belt**. Then Jupiter will come into view. It is an incredible sight! Bands of red, yellow, and white clouds swirl across its surface. The swirling clouds show that Jupiter's **atmosphere** is on the move. Winds howl along at up to 400 miles (650 kilometers) per hour. There are powerful, circular storms and huge lightning flashes.

Once your spaceship starts to **orbit** Jupiter, you will soon realize that the planet is spinning really fast. A day on Jupiter lasts less than 10 hours. This fast spinning is one of the causes of Jupiter's storms.

Jupiter's Great Red Spot is the biggest storm in the solar system. It is three times bigger than Earth and has lasted at least 180 years.

Great Red Spot

Jupiter spins at over 29,204 miles (47,000 kilometers) per hour. If Earth spun at this speed, a day would last less than an hour.

THE BIG CHILL

Jupiter is nearly 500 million miles (800 million kilometers) away from the Sun. Out here it is very cold. The temperature at Jupiter's cloud tops is about –238 degrees Fahrenheit (–150 degrees Celsius).

However, if you tried to land on Jupiter, things would soon start to warm up! The further you go toward the center of the planet, the hotter it gets. At the very center, scientists think the temperature is nearly 72,000 degrees Fahrenheit (40,000 degrees Celsius). This is far hotter than the Sun's surface.

AMAZING FACTS

In 1989, the spacecraft *Galileo* was launched from Earth. It reached Jupiter in 1995. For eight years, *Galileo* orbited Jupiter, gathering information. A lot of what we know about the planet was discovered by *Galileo*.

JUPITER'S MOONS

Your spaceship is not the only thing circling Jupiter. There are also lots of moons. Jupiter has more than 60 of them. The four biggest are called the Galilean moons, because they were first seen by the Italian scientist Galileo in 1610.

Io

The first moon you will visit is Io. It is about the size of Earth's Moon. Our Moon is gray, but Io's surface is yellow, orange, and red. Some people think it looks a little like a pizza! The colors come from chemicals thrown out by erupting volcanoes. There are hundreds of them! You can also see huge lakes of bubbling **molten** rock called lava.

The biggest volcanic eruptions on Io send out plumes of smoke more than 250 miles (400 kilometers) high. You can see one at the top of this photo.

Europa

The whole surface of Europa is covered in ice, crisscrossed with huge cracks. In some areas, the ice has a pinky-brown color, but scientists do not know why. You should not stay long on Europa, because it is a freezing −370 degrees Fahrenheit (−220 degrees Celsius) on the surface. Scientists think that there is a huge ocean, over 62 miles (100 kilometers) deep, beneath the icy crust of Europa. As the icy crust shifts around on the surface of the ocean beneath, this causes cracks in the ice.

Europa is thought to have twice as much water as there is on Earth.

AMAZING FACTS

Scientists want to know for certain what is under Europa's surface. Liquid water is the most important thing needed for life. If Europa has a vast ocean, it is possible that some form of alien life could exist there.

Ganymede and Callisto

The next moon you should visit is Ganymede. This is the biggest moon in the solar system. It is even bigger than the planet Mercury. The surface of Ganymede is icy and dotted with many **craters**. Ganymede has its own **magnetic field**, like Earth, but it is too weak for a **compass** to work well.

Beyond Ganymede is Callisto. Its surface is a mixture of ice and rock. Callisto is covered with millions of craters. It has more craters than any other planet or moon in our solar system. Most of these were caused by **meteorites** that hit the moon billions of years ago. Callisto's surface has hardly changed in all that time, so the marks of these ancient craters are still there.

Jupiter

Europa

Io

Ganymede

Callisto

Ganymede and Callisto are larger than Io and Europa. This picture compares the moons' sizes, but it does not show their actual positions.

HOT ON THE INSIDE

Jupiter's moons are cold on the surface, but below ground some are much hotter. Io is hot enough to produce lava, and Europa has liquid water. All this heat is produced by a combination of gravity and **friction**. As the moons go around Jupiter, the planet's strong gravity pulls on them. However, the moons pull on each other, too. With Jupiter pulling one way and the other moons pulling another, the rocks are constantly being stretched and squeezed. This produces a kind of friction that heats the moons up inside.

NUMBER CRUNCHING

Most of Jupiter's moons are much smaller than the four Galilean moons, and they orbit farther out.

	Diameter in miles/km	Distance from Jupiter in miles/km
Io	2,264 (3,643)	262,094 (421,800)
Europa	1,940 (3,122)	417,002 (671,100)
Ganymede	3,270 (5,262)	665,116 (1,070,400)
Callisto	2,996 (4,821)	1,169,856 (1,882,700)
Himalia	114 (184)	7,121,535 (11,461,000)
Cyllene	1.2 (2)	15,129,767 (24,349,000)

A SYSTEM OF RINGS

It is a long trip to Saturn, but it is worth it to see this beautiful planet up close. Saturn is the second-biggest planet in the solar system. Like all the gas giants, Saturn is made mostly of hydrogen and helium.

The southern part of the planet is creamy gold, turning to a bluish color in the north. The surface has faint stripes, and it looks calmer than Jupiter. But, in fact, the winds can be up to 1,050 miles (1,700 kilometers) per hour!

This photo from 2011, taken by the *Cassini* space probe, shows a storm racing through Saturn's atmosphere.

RIDING THE RINGS

Saturn's rings form a wide band around the **equator**. Saturn's two biggest rings are separated by a gap called the Cassini Division. There are also several much thinner or fainter bands. When the spaceship moves in for a closer look, you will realize that the rings are made of billions of pieces of ice, dust, and rocks. Some pieces are tiny, but a few are as big as mountains.

AMAZING FACTS

Saturn is less **dense** than water. If you could find a bath big enough, the planet would float!

WHO'S WHO?

Christiaan Huygens was a Dutch scientist and astronomer in the 1600s. He observed Saturn through a powerful telescope he designed himself. In 1655, he was the first person to describe Saturn's rings and observe and describe Saturn's moon, Titan.

SATURN'S MOONS

We know a lot about Saturn's moons because of the spacecraft *Cassini*, which reached Saturn in 2004. *Cassini* dropped a probe called *Huygens* onto the surface of Saturn's largest moon. Now you are going to follow *Huygens*.

Titan

Titan is the only moon in the solar system known to have a thick atmosphere. Small moons do not usually have enough gravity to keep an atmosphere. The gases escape into space. The low temperatures on Titan mean that gases are thicker and escape less easily than on Earth. But we do not know why Titan has a thick atmosphere, when Ganymede and Callisto, which are similar, do not.

This is what scientists think the surface of Titan might look like, with its lakes of liquid methane and thick, orange fog.

Titan's atmosphere is thick, and the whole moon seems to be covered in orange fog. There are valleys on Titan and lakes, but the liquid in the lakes is not water—it is **methane**. On Earth, methane is a gas. We use it for cooking and heating. But on Titan, it is so cold that methane acts like water. It even rains methane on the surface. The raindrops are bigger than raindrops on Earth, and they fall slowly, because Titan's gravity is weak.

NUMBER CRUNCHING

Here are the key facts about Saturn.

DIAMETER:
74,900 miles (120,500 kilometers)

DISTANCE FROM SUN:
886,500,000 miles
(1,426,700,000 kilometers)

LENGTH OF YEAR:
29.5 Earth years

DAY LENGTH:
10 hours, 40 minutes

NUMBER OF MOONS:
at least 63

After you have visited Titan, perhaps you will have time to fly past another of Saturn's moon, Mimas. If you do, take a look at Mimas's enormous crater! It is named Herschel Crater, after the astronomer William Herschel (see page 22).

Enceladus

After visiting Titan, you might want to head for a much smaller moon called Enceladus. The surface of Enceladus is covered in ice. The average surface temperature is –330 degrees Fahrenheit (–200 degrees Celsius). This is so cold that it would turn Earth's atmosphere into a liquid. But one area seems to be much warmer—it will be an interesting place to go down and investigate.

The warm area turns out to be at the South **Pole**! The heat is coming from several wide valleys running alongside each other. If you land close to one of them and look out of the window, you will see big plumes of bright, white ice spraying upward. The ice in these incredible fountains does not fall back to the ground. It continues its path upward, going thousands of miles into space.

Huge jets of ice shoot up from the surface of Enceladus. The ice from these plumes forms a faint outer ring called the E ring.

What causes these incredible jets? Like Io and Europa, Enceladus is squeezed by gravity as it orbits Saturn. This heats up the ice underground, and some of it melts. In the valleys at the south pole of Enceladus, the surface ice is thin. Cracks form, and water from under the ground shoots out at high speed. Above ground, the water freezes and turns into a fountain of ice.

Saturn is not the only planet to have rings. All the other gas giants have them, too. Saturn's rings are icy and reflect sunlight. The rings of the other planets are thinner and made of dark rock or ice. This makes them much harder to see.

If you have time, fly past Iapetus, another of Saturn's moons. Iapetus is unusual because it has a very dark side and a very bright side.

INTERVIEW WITH A SPACE SCIENTIST

John Spencer works on **NASA's** Cassini mission, which is exploring Saturn and its moons. His team plans where the *Cassini* spacecraft will go and what information it will gather.

Q *How long is the radio delay between Earth and Saturn?*

A It varies, but it is about an hour and a half. So you certainly can't control the spacecraft in real time. You plan everything out in advance, and you send up instructions that you will have figured out probably a month or more in advance.

Q *When Cassini is doing a fly-by of a moon, how long do you have to look at it?*

A Well, we're going very fast and some of these moons are quite small. When we are flying past Enceladus it really just takes a couple of minutes from one side of the moon to the other. It's like barreling down the road and trying to read a mile post at the side of the road and you're doing 60 miles an hour.

Q *What is the most exciting or interesting thing that the mission has learned so far?*

A For me, it's the activity on the moon Enceladus. We have these fractures, with the heat coming out of the interior. We are seeing such warm temperatures there—and we are seeing such energy coming out of the interior—that we think there may be liquid water not very far below the surface. That would be really exciting, because liquid water is so rare in the solar system, and where there is liquid water, there is a chance that life might have developed.

Q *If you had the opportunity to go anywhere in space, is there anywhere in particular that you would like to visit in person?*

A If you could get around these little problems like catching on fire, Titan would be a fascinating place to explore. I would love to be there for one of the methane thunderstorms and see the rivers filling up and waterfalls of liquid methane rushing down to the lakes. Or to be on Enceladus and see these **geysers** that are coming out of the ground at tremendous speed. The view of Saturn you would get from there would be astonishing.

Q *Have you always wanted a career in space?*

A I think since the Apollo days I really have been very excited about space, but it took me a while to come to the realization that, yeah, you can get paid to do this stuff! The stuff we get to do—we have this spaceship, and it's a real spaceship! And it's flying around the planet Saturn! We get to control it! It's kind of mind-boggling to me—I still have to pinch myself sometimes.

BLUE NEIGHBORS

Going from Saturn to Uranus is a very long trip. Uranus is almost 2 billion miles (3 billion kilometers) from the Sun— twice as far away as Saturn. As your spaceship flies on, the Sun will seem to get smaller and smaller.

At last, Uranus will appear up ahead. The planet is almost completely blue-green. This color comes from small amounts of methane in the atmosphere. There are faint stripes on the surface, as on Saturn. But the stripes on Uranus seem to run up and down, rather than side to side.

NUMBER CRUNCHING

Uranus is really cold. The temperature can drop to −366 degrees Fahrenheit (−221 degrees Celsius). Uranus is colder than any other planet.

William Herschel discovered Uranus in 1781.

ON ITS SIDE

Normally, a planet spins so that one side faces the Sun, then the other. As the planet goes around, it changes from day to night, and back again. But Uranus does not spin like this. It is tilted on its side, which makes the days and seasons very complicated.

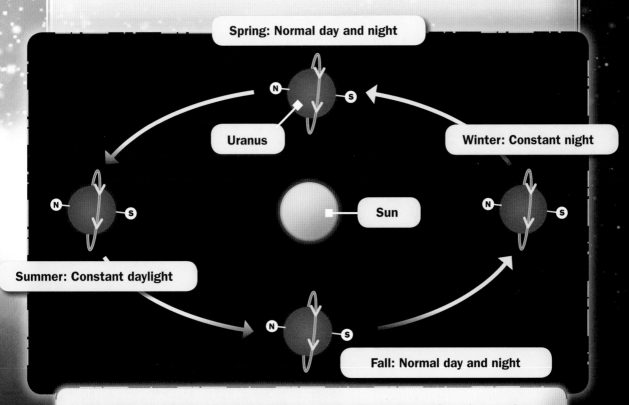

Spring: Normal day and night

Uranus

Winter: Constant night

Sun

Summer: Constant daylight

Fall: Normal day and night

This diagram shows the changing seasons in Uranus's southern hemisphere.

AMAZING FACTS

A year on Uranus is 84 Earth years long. This means that if you lived on Uranus, you might only orbit the Sun once in your whole lifetime!

DARK RINGS

As your spaceship flies around Uranus, you will faintly see its rings above you. The ring system of Uranus was discovered by accident. Several U.S. astronomers were watching as Uranus passed in front of a star. They were hoping to learn something about the planet's atmosphere as the star lit it from behind. As Uranus came close, the star got dim and then bright again five times. The same thing happened on the other side, as Uranus moved away.

The best explanation was that Uranus had five dark rings circling it. Since then, more rings have been found. Scientists think that the rings may be the remains of a moon that smashed to pieces millions of years ago.

This computer-colored picture shows Uranus and its rings. The bright spots outside the rings are moons.

MOON VISITS

Uranus has 27 known moons. If you do not have time to visit them all, you should visit two of the larger ones, Miranda and Titania. Both are cold and dark, but the landscapes are amazing. Miranda has huge areas of tumbled rock, jagged ridges, and deep canyons. On Titania, there is a huge canyon that is 994 miles (1,600 kilometers) long.

This photo, taken by the *Voyager* space probe, shows the giant grooves on Titania's surface.

Alexis Bouvard was a French mathematician and astronomer. In 1821, he used all the information available at the time to calculate the orbit of Uranus. However, the calculations did not match the planet's actual position. Bouvard predicted that Uranus's orbit was being affected by another, unknown planet. His ideas eventually led to the discovery of Neptune in 1846.

AN OCEAN OF GAS

The trip to Neptune takes even longer than the path from Saturn to Uranus. On average, Neptune is 2.8 billion miles (4.5 billion kilometers) from the Sun. By the time you arrive, the Sun will be so far away it will look like no more than a bright star.

Neptune is a beautiful bright blue. You can see light and dark bands, flecks of white, and some dark patches. The dark patches are huge storms. Winds on the planet reach an incredible 1,567 miles (2,520 kilometers) per hour. The fastest winds on Earth only reach 231 miles (372 kilometers) per hour.

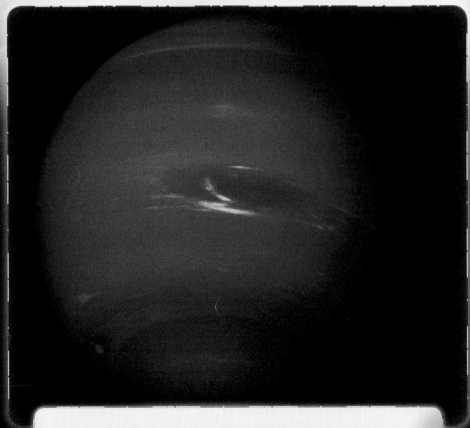

Stormy Neptune is nearly four times the size of Earth.

NEPTUNE'S MOONS

After spending some time weather-watching, you should make a quick tour of Neptune's moons. Neptune has 13 moons, but most of them are small and oddly shaped. The only one worth landing on is Triton.

Triton's surface has mountains and valleys, flat plains, craters, and some odd dark streaks on the surface. There are also wispy clouds. Triton has an atmosphere! Try to land your spaceship close to one of the dark streaks on the surface. Huge geysers spray out a mixture of nitrogen gas and dust. The dust settles downwind, causing the dark streaks.

Here, Neptune can be seen on the horizon of its moon, Triton. The image was made from information sent back to Earth by the *Voyager 2* spacecraft (see page 30).

After Neptune, you will be heading back to Earth. Before you go, you look out into the blackness. Is there anything beyond Neptune?

It will be a long, hard journey to get back to Earth after visiting Neptune. Head toward the Sun to find your way.

AMAZING FACTS

In 1930, a small, icy object was spotted orbiting beyond Neptune. It was called the planet Pluto. Pluto was tiny, and it had an oval-shaped orbit. Astronomers wondered if it should count as a planet. In 2005, another object called Eris was discovered. It was bigger than Pluto. Scientists have now decided that Pluto and Eris are both dwarf planets.

THE KUIPER BELT

For many years, only the **dwarf planet** Pluto was known to orbit beyond Neptune. However, many astronomers believed there was a broad band of icy **asteroids** beyond Neptune, which they called the **Kuiper Belt**. In 1992, the first Kuiper Belt Object (KBO) was discovered. Since then, astronomers have found hundreds of KBOs, and there are probably billions more.

A CLOUD OF COMETS

Far beyond the Kuiper Belt is another, much bigger cloud of icy pieces called the Oort Cloud. Many of the **comets** that we occasionally see in the sky come from here.

The nearest stars are far beyond the Oort Cloud. Beyond them there are even more stars. We are part of a huge whirl of stars in space—the Milky Way **galaxy**. Beyond the Milky Way are billions more galaxies. This is the **universe**.

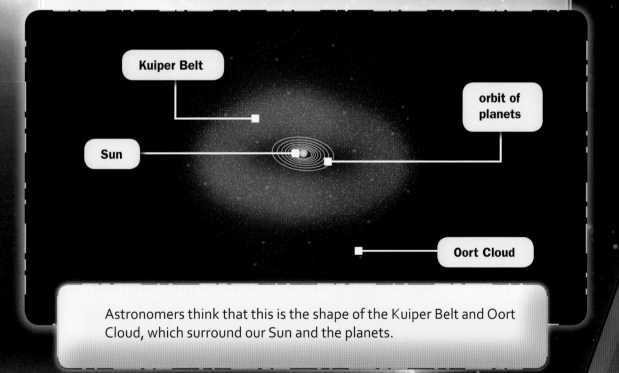

Astronomers think that this is the shape of the Kuiper Belt and Oort Cloud, which surround our Sun and the planets.

Is a trip to Neptune actually possible? We have the technology to get there—the *Voyager 2* spacecraft made the trip. In 2006, another space probe was launched, called *New Horizons*. It is on course to reach Neptune in just eight years.

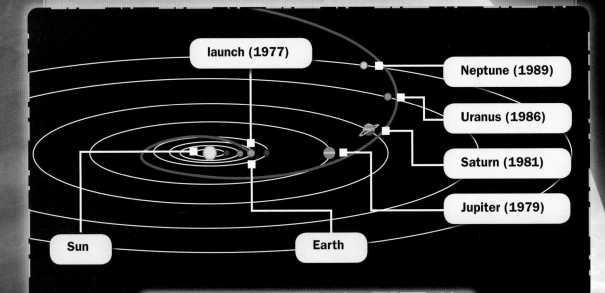

launch (1977)

Neptune (1989)

Uranus (1986)

Saturn (1981)

Jupiter (1979)

Sun

Earth

Voyager 2 took 12 years to reach Neptune.

The big problem is building a spaceship that can carry people. The *New Horizons* probe weighs only 1,054 pounds (478 kilograms). The spacecraft that took astronauts to the Moon was 100 times heavier! And they needed only a few days' supplies, while you would need enough food for years.

FOOD AND FUEL

Even with powdered food, it would be hard to carry enough supplies for such a long trip. However, it might be possible to grow food on the way. Scientists on the **International Space Station (ISS)** are researching ways to grow plants in space.

Another big problem is power. Rockets use a lot of fuel, so you would need huge fuel tanks to get to Neptune. An answer to this might be a kind of engine called an ion motor. This uses electricity to turn a small amount of gas into a jet shooting out of the motor. Ion motors take a long time to get a spacecraft going, but once they do, they are incredibly fast.

DON'T FORGET

One of the essentials on a long space trip is water. The ISS has a water recovery system that can recycle 92 percent of waste water. For a trip to the outer planets, even more water would have to be recovered.

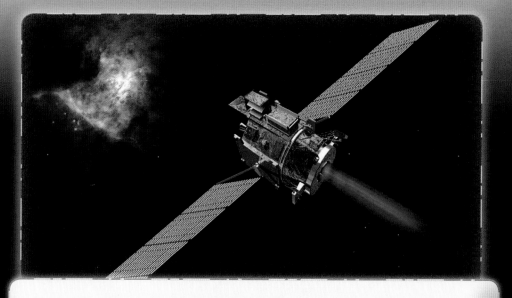

Ion thrusters have already been used for some spacecraft, like this one for the *Deep Space* probe.

WHO'S GOING WITH YOU?

Suppose you solve all the problems and actually build your spaceship. Who would you want to come with you? Here are some ideas.

CREW MEMBER:

GALILEO GALILEI (1564–1642)
The Italian Galileo was one of the greatest scientists of all time. He made very good telescopes, so he could probably fix things if they stopped working correctly. He knew a lot about Jupiter: he was the first to see its biggest moons.

POTENTIAL JOB:
Mission commander

CREW MEMBER:

GIAN DOMENICO CASSINI (1625–1712)
Cassini was also Italian, but he was a Saturn specialist. The gap in Saturn's rings is named after him, and he discovered four of Saturn's moons.

POTENTIAL JOB:
Chief astronomer

CREW MEMBER:

WILLIAM HERSCHEL (1738–1822)

Herschel was a German scientist who moved to England. He built amazing telescopes. He discovered Uranus, so he would be good on the later part of the trip.

POTENTIAL JOB:

Chief scientist

CREW MEMBER:

CAROLYN PORCO (BORN 1953)

U.S. scientist Porco is an expert on the outer planets. She worked on the Voyager missions in the 1980s, and since 2004 she has been in charge of the team working on the incredible pictures of Saturn and its moons from the *Cassini* spacecraft.

POTENTIAL JOB:

Imaging specialist

CREW MEMBER:

ROALD AMUNDSEN (1872–1928)

The Norwegian Amundsen led the first team of explorers to reach the South Pole, so he knew a lot about surviving the cold. He was also interested in flying and led an expedition to the North Pole by airship.

POTENTIAL JOB:

Survival expert

INTERVIEW WITH AN ASTRONAUT

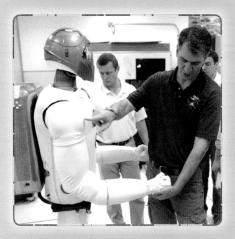

Paolo Nespoli is an Italian astronaut with the **European Space Agency (ESA)**. In 2007, Paolo went into space for 15 days, and in 2010 he spent 6 more months in space. In total, he has orbited Earth an amazing 2,782 times.

Q *Your very first trip into space was on a space shuttle. What did it feel like on takeoff? What were you thinking?*

A Going up in space is a risky business in a certain way, because you are strapped to a car that is going up in space propelled almost by an atomic explosion ... And on top of that you have to add the fact that you don't just go up for a fun ride—you go up to accomplish something, to accomplish some goals which are technically challenging and complex. So what I actually felt was, on one side, some kind of happiness that the long wait and the long training was finished—this was the real thing. On the other side, I felt a little bit of apprehension. Would I perform properly as I was requested to? Would everything be okay, or would I make a mistake about something? But everything went pretty well. You go up and nothing happens, you just enjoy the ride. It is quite an amazing feeling.

Q *You worked with Robonaut on the International Space Station. Do you think that robots like that could ever replace human astronauts?*

A Well, the straight answer is no … or it's going to be very difficult. Robonaut and robots in space are extremely useful. So I think it's not a question of replacing, I think it's a question of working together, because there are a lot of activities on the station that we did that are very tedious. Little things, little operations that have to be repeated a dozen times or more … it's much, much better if a robot were able to do that activity. They are really precise, they don't complain, they don't go to the bathroom or things like that.

Q *How about humans—how do you use the bathroom in space?*

A I go to the bathroom the same way I go here—maybe I float to the bathroom there instead of walking to the bathroom, but it's only the technical part that is a little bit different. There is equipment there which essentially traps solids and fluids—obviously, there are certain things that you don't want to float around on the spacecraft! It's like a regular toilet that we have here, the only thing that's different is that it has to contain these things. It's not anything fancy, it's just a big vacuum cleaner that vacuums up stuff and then stores it and then we throw away the containers.

FUTURE EXPLORATIONS

There have been real space missions to the outer planets in the past. Some new missions are already under way, and more are planned for the future. For example, the New Horizons mission is the first that was designed to fly beyond the planets. It has already flown past Jupiter and sent back detailed photos of its atmosphere. In 2015, it will reach Pluto, then it will go on to visit other Kuiper Belt Objects.

This is what *New Horizons* will look like as it reaches Pluto. The spacecraft's huge dish antenna will let it communicate with Earth from billions of miles away.

JUNO

Another major mission to the outer planets blasted off in 2011. The *Juno* spacecraft is heading for Jupiter, where it will peer deep into the atmosphere. It should arrive in 2016. *Juno* is one of the biggest and heaviest spacecraft sent to explore the planets. It weighs over 3 tons.

Voyager and other spacecraft flying to the outer planets were powered by **nuclear** batteries. These used **radioactive** fuel to produce electricity. *Juno* gets its power from sunlight. It has three enormous **solar panels**, because the sunlight close to Jupiter is much weaker than here on Earth.

European and Russian space scientists are planning a mission to send two spacecraft to Jupiter and its moons. One of these spacecraft will orbit Jupiter's largest moon, Ganymede. The other spacecraft will orbit Europa and send a lander down onto the surface. The two missions are due to launch in 2020.

It will take five years for *Juno* to reach Jupiter. When it gets there, *Juno* will orbit Jupiter 33 times.

COULD WE LIVE THERE?

You have been a tourist to the outer planets. But would you like to live there? One thing is certain—humans could not live on the gas giants. If you were not frozen at the cloud tops, you might get blown away by a storm or fried by lighting. But what about some of the moons?

WATER FOR LIFE

The most important thing for the survival of living things is water. Without water, we could not live anywhere for long. Many of the moons of Jupiter and Saturn are icy, and a lot of this ice is water. On Europa and Enceladus, there might even be hidden oceans. These moons are far colder than Earth, but there seems to be heat below the surface. It might be possible to generate electricity from this heat. We really might be able to live there.

A HOME FOR LIFE

What scientists find exciting is that there could already be living things on Europa or Enceladus. Life on Earth began in the ocean. So it is possible that there could be simple living things in the ocean below Europa. On Earth, there are tiny **bacteria** that can live in ice and others that live around the edges of hot geysers shooting from the ground. Perhaps there are living things around the icy geysers on Enceladus?

If there was life on these moons, it would be incredible. We have spent years looking for aliens among the stars. Compared to those huge distances, alien life on Saturn's moons would be almost at our doorstep.

This is what it might look like if humans set up a base on our Moon. We would need a lot of special equipment to be able to live on another moon or planet. Perhaps it could really happen in the future!

ASTEROID BELT

JUPITER

SATURN

URANUS

NEPTUNE

The sizes of the planets and their distances from the Sun are not to scale. To show all the planets' real distances from the Sun, this page would have to be over half a mile long!

TIMELINE

362 BCE Chinese astronomer Gan De may have observed one of Jupiter's moons.

1609–1610 Italian scientist Galileo Galilei discovers four Galilean moons.

1655 Dutch scientist Christiaan Huygens is the first to identify Saturn's rings. He also discovers Saturn's largest moon, Titan.

1675 Gian Domenico Cassini, an Italian–French astronomer, discovers a narrow gap in Saturn's rings. It is named the Cassini Division after him.

1781 British astronomer William Herschel discovers Uranus. At first, he thinks that it is a comet.

1846 Two astronomers, John Adams in Great Britain and Urbain LeVerrier in France, predict the position of a previously unknown planet. German astronomer Johann Galle finds the planet Neptune almost exactly where predicted.
English businessman and astronomer William Lassell discovers Neptune's moon Triton.

1948 U.S. astronomer Gerard Kuiper discovers Uranus's moon, Miranda.

1949 Gerard Kuiper suggests that a belt of comets exists beyond the planets. It is now called the Kuiper Belt. He also predicts that Saturn's rings are made of ice and discovers Nereid (one of Neptune's moons).

1977–present The *Voyager 1* and *Voyager 2* flights are launched in 1977. *Voyager 1* reaches Jupiter in 1979 and Saturn in 1980. *Voyager 2* flies past Uranus in 1986 and Neptune in 1989.

1989–2003 The *Galileo* space mission flies to Jupiter and visits the Galilean moons. It releases a small probe into Jupiter's atmosphere in 1995; over the next five years, the probe visits Io, Europa, Ganymede, and Callisto. It deliberately crashes into Jupiter in 2003.

1997–present The spacecraft *Cassini* and space probe *Huygens* begin a mission to Saturn and its moons in 1997. *Cassini* reaches Saturn in 2004; the *Huygens* probe lands on Titan in 2005.

2006–2007 The space probe *New Horizons* launches in 2006 and flies past Jupiter in 2007.

2015
New Horizons is due to reach the dwarf planet Pluto.

JUPITER	SATURN	URANUS	NEPTUNE
Average distance from Sun: 483,600,000 mi. (778,300,000 km)	**Average distance from Sun:** 886,500,000 mi. (1,426,700,000 km)	**Average distance from Sun:** 1,783,700,000 mi. (2,870,700,000 km)	**Average distance from Sun:** 2,795,200,000 mi. (4,498,400,000 km)
Diameter: 88,800 mi. (143,000 km)	**Diameter:** 74,900 mi. (120,500 km)	**Diameter:** 31,700 mi. (51,100 km)	**Diameter:** 30,700 mi. (49,500 km)
Number of known moons: 64	**Number of known moons:** At least 62	**Number of known moons:** 27	**Number of known moons:** 13
Length of day: 9.9 Earth hours	**Length of day:** 10.6 Earth hours	**Length of day:** 17.2 Earth hours	**Length of day:** 16.1 Earth hours
Length of year: 11.9 Earth years	**Length of year:** 29.4 Earth years	**Length of year:** 84.0 Earth years	**Length of year:** 164.8 Earth years
Temperature: −234 °F (−148 °C)	**Temperature:** −288 °F (−178 °C)	**Temperature:** −357 °F (−216 °C)	**Temperature:** −353 °F (−214 °C)
Mainly made from: Hydrogen, helium	**Mainly made from:** Hydrogen, helium	**Mainly made from:** Hydrogen, helium, methane	**Mainly made from:** Hydrogen, helium, methane

GLOSSARY

asteroid small object in the solar system that is traveling on its own path around the Sun

asteroid belt area between Mars and Jupiter where most asteroids can be found

astronomer person who studies space

atmosphere layer of gases surrounding a planet

bacteria microscopic living things with a very simple structure

comet object made of rock and ice that orbits the Sun. A comet that gets close to the Sun develops a long "tail" of gas and dust.

compass instrument that finds the direction of magnetic north and can be used to find one's way around

crater dish-shaped hole in the surface of a planet, made by a meteorite smashing into the surface

dense made of tightly packed material

dwarf planet planet that is small compared to the main planets

equator imaginary line around the middle of a star or planet

European Space Agency (ESA) European organization involved in space research and exploration

friction force that tries to slow down or stop objects that are rubbing against each other

galaxy huge "island" of stars in space. Our galaxy, the Milky Way, contains at least 10 billion stars.

gas matter, such as oxygen, that is able to expand without limit unless it is contained

geyser hot spring that sometimes erupts, sending a tall column of water and steam into the air

gravity force that pulls objects toward each other. Big objects, such as planets, have much stronger gravity than smaller objects, such as people.

International Space Station (ISS) large spacecraft orbiting Earth on which astronauts from different countries live and work

Kuiper Belt region beyond the orbit of Neptune where many pieces of rock and ice of all sizes orbit the Sun

magnetic field region around a magnet where it has an effect on magnetic materials and other magnets

meteorite piece of space rock or metal

methane natural gas—the gas that we use for cooking, heating, and generating electricity

molten solid that has melted to become liquid

NASA short for "National Aeronautics and Space Administration," the U.S. space agency

nuclear (power) energy generated in the nucleus of an atom

orbit path of an object around a star or planet

pole two regions at the north and south ends of a planet

radioactive producing radiation from nuclear activity

solar panel electronic panel that absorbs sunlight and converts it into electricity

solar system the Sun, the planets, and other objects that are in orbit around the Sun

space probe unmanned spacecraft that is sent to study an object in space

telescope device that makes distant objects look bigger

universe everything that exists, including all of space and all the objects and energy in it

FIND OUT MORE

BOOKS

Aguilar, David A. *13 Planets: The Latest View of the Solar System* (National Geographic Kids). Washington, D.C.: National Geographic, 2011.

Bond, Peter. *DK Guide to Space* (DK Guides). New York: Dorling Kindersley, 2006.

Goldsmith, Mike. *Solar System* (Discover Science). New York: Macmillan, 2010.

Graham, Ian. *What Do We Know About the Solar System?* (Earth, Space, and Beyond). Chicago: Raintree, 2011.

Solway, Andrew. *Why Is There Life on Earth?* (Earth, Space and Beyond). Chicago: Raintree, 2012.

Stott, Carole. *Space: From Earth to the Edge of the Universe*. New York: Dorling Kindersley, 2010.

INTERNET SITES

FactHound offers a safe, fun way to find internet sites related to this book. All of the sites on FactHound have been researched by our staff.

Here's all you do:

Visit *www.facthound.com*

Type in this code: 9781410945693

DVDS

A Traveler's Guide to the Planets (National Geographic, 2010)
The Universe (A&E, 2010)

PLACES TO VISIT

Hayden Planetarium
Central Park West and 79th Street, New York, N.Y. 10024
www.haydenplanetarium.org

Jet Propulsion Laboratory
4800 Oak Grove Drive, Pasadena, California 9110
www.jpl.nasa.gov

Kennedy Space Center
SR 405, Kennedy Space Center, Florida 32899
www.nasa.gov/centers/kennedy

Smithsonian National Air and Space Museum
Independence Ave. at 7th St. SW, Washington, D.C. 20560
www.nasm.si.edu

FURTHER RESEARCH

Here are some starting points for finding out more about the outer planets:

- Find out more about the *New Directions* space probe. Where is it now? When is the next landmark in its flight?
- There were once nine planets in our solar system. Can you find out about Pluto, the ninth planet? Who discovered it, and when? Does it have any moons?